Peanut Butter, Playdates & Prozac
Tales from a Modern Mom

Arlene Schusteff

Wyatt-MacKenzie Publishing, Inc.
DEADWOOD, OREGON

Peanut Butter, Playdates & Prozac:
Tales from a Modern Mom
by Arlene Schusteff

Photography by Mindy Garfinkle.

Published by The Mom-Writers Publishing Cooperative
Wyatt-MacKenzie Publishing, Inc., Deadwood, OR
www.WyMacPublishing.com (541) 964-3314

Cover Illustration: Kelley Cunningham, kelleysart.com

Requests for permission or further information should be addressed to:
Wyatt-MacKenzie Publishing, 15115 Highway 36,
Deadwood, Oregon 97430

Printed in the United States of America

Peanut Butter,
Playdates & Prozac
Tales from a Modern Mom

Arlene Schusteff

Dedication

This book is dedicated to my mom, who always told me that one day I'd be dedicating a book to her. Okay, so you were right!

Acknowledgements

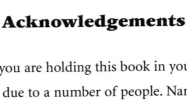

The fact that you are holding this book in your hand is in no small part due to a number of people. Nancy Cleary, thanks for holding my hand, putting up with all my questions and believing in me and this book. MWPC gals, you all are the best!

Mom, Norm, Bubbie and Papa, I love you even when you don't babysit. Without you, there would be no Rachel and Jake.

Danny, I wrote a book and you didn't. Ha! Ha! Guess I'm the favorite one now!

Sue, Adriane, Bonnie, Wendy, Jenny, Gerri, Ruth, Gail, Rhonda, Sarah, Karyn, Maggie, Debi, Amy, Dhana, and Andrea, thank you for keeping me stocked with chocolate and driving my share of the carpools. I promise, none of this is about you! Well, almost none of it.

Howard, once the kids slept through the night, your snoring kept me up and thinking of funny stories at 3:00 a.m. I guess in retrospect I'm glad you never got the Breathe Right strips. Seriously, thanks for taking the kids to Nickel City so that I could write and always supporting me. I love you.

Rachel and Jake, Jake and Rachel, (see, you were both first. It's fair!). You are my inspiration. When you finally decide to read this book, remember, we're laughing with you not at you. I love you both.

Table of Contents

Introduction

Not sure this book is for you? Let me help…..

Have you ever bribed your children to let you talk on the phone?

Have you ever lied about being busy to avoid a PTA commitment?

Do you have a garbage bag full of Happy Meal toys in your basement?

Have you ever hid your cell phone bill from your husband so he wouldn't ask you why you have so much time to "talk on the phone all day?"

Have you ever told your kids that baseball practice, dance or soccer was cancelled because you were too lazy to drive them?

Does your family give you a standing ovation when you cook dinner?

Are the squares on your calendar too small to fit in all the activities, appointments and playdates?

Do you secretly dread snow days, school holidays and chaperoning field trips?

Have you ever threatened to call *SuperNanny* if they didn't behave?

Are you a mom?

If you answered yes to two or more of these questions, welcome! You're among friends. And, you're in good company. There are quite a few of us re-gifting the toy gun our kid got for a birthday present and trying to ditch the PTA president at the grocery store. We're pretty easy to spot. We're the ones who give in and buy our whining kid a lollipop at 8 am just to shut him up. Sometimes we do actually cry over spilled milk. Often, our days are too long and our tempers are too short. But, when push comes to shove (which in my house it usually does) we wouldn't change a thing. Well, not too many things anyway.

So, pop in a long DVD, give them some snacks and enjoy. Like I said, you're among friends.

Kid 101

There are hundreds, maybe thousands of books devoted to giving new moms advice. Well-meaning friends and relatives can be counted on to give you their expert opinions on raising children. So, why should you listen to me? I am certainly no esteemed expert. (One look at my kids will verify that!). But, I am a little less annoying than your mother-in-law and a lot more honest than all those helpful books. As my mother once said (more advice!) "Learn from my mistakes." Just don't shoot the messenger.

Sleep

You will not sleep. Not ever. Once you come to terms with this fact, life will be easier. You will not spend your waking hours (which is all of them) obsessing about whether or not the baby is sleeping and trying to get her to sleep so that you can sleep. Just remember the sleep motto: It's always something. When you consider teething, gas, croup, night terrors, potty training, time changes, monsters under the bed and ugly pajamas (no joke) you will pray for the one night a week you manage to get a few hours shut eye. When you're at your wits end and have tried Ferber, Weissbluth and Leach, consider the following... According to my informal survey, most Kindergarteners are sleeping through the night. Oh, and here's a bonus tip: If you meet a mom at the mall who insists "her child slept through at six weeks," do not, under any circumstances, invite her to join your playgroup.

Food

Too much, not enough. The debate rages on. Is there ever a day where little precious eats exactly the right amount of food? Bottle and breast is bad enough. Wait till the toddler years. Toddler's have their own hierarchy of food, and believe me, it has nothing to do with any pyramid. Two helpful phrases are key to remember here; "No, McDonald's is closed today" and "The grocery store does not sell candy in the morning. It's a law."

Manners and Discipline

Ever notice how people without children are experts on how to get yours to behave? I'd like to follow up with the woman pregnant with triplets who told me that "she's going to teach them manners when they are really young so that they will learn how to behave right from the get-go." (Are you laughing yet?) Or the friend who told me that she's not going to use television as a babysitter. Ha! Which brings us to our next area....

Television

I know, you're not going to use the electronic babysitter with your kids. Consider the following scenario: You've had a bad day. Lot's of bodily fluids and not enough sleep. It is 5:30 p.m. Husband missed his train, won't be home for another two hours. Pasta is boiling over. Baby is crying and won't take the propped up bottle. Wants you. Now. Toddler is demanding to finger paint. If you are even considering dropping everything (No, not the baby!) to finger paint with little Picasso, I have not done my job. Grab a DVD. Fast. Enough said.

Development

Your child's development will progress in inverse proportion to how worried you are about it. If you are one of the lucky (Ha!) mothers whose child walks at nine months, please don't brag to the rest of us. If you do, we're likely to pay you back when he is five and wants to take his binky to Kindergarten!

Dress

I am referring to both you and the baby. First you. You have earned the right to wear sweatpants and a stained tee-shirt for the next six months. You do not need a "New Mom Makeover." Ignore magazine articles that tell you you'll feel better if you put on a cute blazer, jeans and heels. You won't. This is absolutely the only time you can dress like crap for months on end and no one will talk about you. Relish it. In terms of the baby, take the hand-me-downs!

The baby doesn't know what it's wearing! Save your money. Before you know it, little precious will be demanding North Face jackets and Ugg boots.

And, finally, I leave you with the best advice anyone ever gave me. Surprisingly enough, it came from a stranger. I was waiting in line at the grocery store with my shrieking baby and whining toddler. The other people in line (Mothers, can you believe it?) were shooting me daggers. One suggested that it would be easier to shop if I left my children at home, (Duh. Like I would choose this if I had a choice!). It was almost my turn when an elderly woman approached us to have a look at "my beautiful kids." Her words still resonate with me today. "Don't listen to what other people say, it's all rubbish," she said in a stage whisper. "Just smile, nod your head and then do whatever you damn well please." Amen.

Starbucks Stepfords

Let me say this right in the beginning. I can quit anytime I want. Really, I can. Once I even drank instant
coffee when I was at my in-laws house. I know that if
I saved up all the money I spent on Starbucks and
brewed my own, I could afford to send one kid to
college. And, if I ever forget that fact, my husband is
quick to remind me.

But, I kind of look at it this way. My figure is gone.
I have stretch marks. I watch SpongeBob and Mary
Kate and Ashley movies. I am a room mother. I take
other peoples kids with me to dinner, movies and the
park. I am on call 24/7. I clean up throw up and wipe
noses. I deserve a good cup of coffee!!

If I walk into Starbucks at 8:45, right after the kids get
dropped at school, I am guaranteed a friendly greet-
ing by someone not calling me MOOOOOMMMMY.
I am allowed, and even encouraged, to be picky about

my drink. Yes, it's me being picky, not them! I am handed my drink with a smile and asked if I would like anything else. The napkins and stirrers and milk and cream are neat and organized. Everything is predictable and I am in control. No one needs me.

I see others just like me. We smile at each other in recognition. We stream in all morning, like soldier's getting their ammunition.

I walk out to the parking lot and see all the vans lined up in a row. I drive to the grocery store and put my green and white cup in the cup-holder of the cart. When I see another mother sipping and shopping, we smile at each other. We are all over. There's a huge cluster of us over in the frozen foods section. The cups appear to have become an extension of our hand. We never put them down. Never.

Right before I check out, I drain the cup and look for a garbage. I find one, overflowing with the telltale green and white cups. Back to reality, I think. Then I wonder, just what the heck are they putting in that coffee anyway?

Eight Surefire Ways to Make a Moms Blood Boil
A Primer for Children

After waiting in line for an hour to see a movie, watch the previews and then announce, "I'm bored, I want to go".

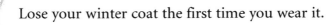

Lose your winter coat the first time you wear it.

When you're in the bathtub, let the water overflow so it leaks into the kitchen below.

Walk over and around the towel on the bathroom floor. Do not, under any circumstance, pick it up.

Never speak in a normal voice. Whine, yell, or better yet, mimic everything mom says.

Never use a tissue. Wipe your nose on the sofa, a dishtowel, or the backseat of the car.

Insist that the new shoes feel great in the store. Then, wear them to school the next day and tell mom they hurt and you're never wearing them again.

After mom gets home from the supermarket, tell her you need brownies for the bake sale...tomorrow.

Actual Conversation

(Rachel, at age five)

(Relayed to me with only mild amusement
by preschool teacher at conference time)

Teacher: Rachel, please put the blocks away.

Teacher: Rachel, please put the blocks away.

Rachel: I'm not the maid, you know.

Your Mother Said You'd Understand

Now you know that…

Wet towels in the hamper do matter.

A little lipstick does brighten up your whole face.

It is a good idea to separate the whites and the darks.

The weight is harder to lose as you get older.

Manners do count.

"Because I said so" is reason enough.

Jobs I'm Uniquely Qualified for After Raising Children

Fortune Teller

Able to see into the future with absolute certainty. Once predicted which child would get sick on vacation and which child would ultimately drop the beer mug she insisted on using for her milk.

Union Negotiator

If you get your homework done you can stay up for 10 extra minutes. You only want to read, fine, go ahead and read. Yes, that does count as the 10 minutes. I know its reading but it still counts, you don't get an extra 10 minutes after the reading. No, like I said, it is the same 10 minutes.

Short Order Cook

So let me see if I have this straight: One grilled cheese, no butter, no crust, on white. One cup of noodles, sauce on the side. One peanut butter and jelly, no jelly, just peanut butter on both sides of the bread cut in a diagonal. One milk, one water no ice, one lemonade watered down.

Quality Control Manager for Snack Food Company

Can tell if portion is bigger by eyeing it. Honed skills by dishing out the exact number of Cheerios and M&Ms to each kid.

Hazardous Waste Cleaner

Able to clean up any bodily fluid with a cloth diaper, or in a pinch, a sock.

Magician

Can make children disappear instantly by asking them to help clean up.

Seven Wonders of a Modern Mom's World

1. Mommy Time – It can move slow or fast depending on what you're doing. Runs in inverse proportion to the enjoyment of your activity.

2. Your children have the ability to program themselves to get sick the weekend they're supposed to stay at grandmas.

3. The only time a drink spills is when it's chocolate milk or grape juice.

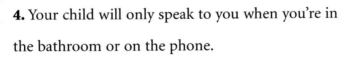

4. Your child will only speak to you when you're in the bathroom or on the phone.

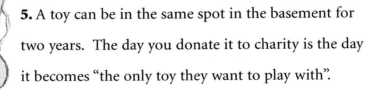

5. A toy can be in the same spot in the basement for two years. The day you donate it to charity is the day it becomes "the only toy they want to play with".

6. The same child that is physically unable to make her bed can program the DVD player and mail merge your holiday card list.

7. The moment you decide your child is old enough to walk to school alone, she refuses to.

Schoolmarms

Go to Any Elementary School and I'm Willing to Bet You'll Find…

The Hot Mama (aka "I'm Too Sexy for My Shirt")
This hot mama attends PTA meetings in low-rise jeans, heels, and a fitted cami. Knows the name of every husband in the school. Dresses up as a belly dancer for the school Halloween party.

The Martha Stewart on Speed
Bakes for every bake sale (and we're not talking slice and dice). Sews her kids Halloween costumes. Has an immaculate house with a cutting garden and no toys on the front lawn.

The Competitor
Sends an email blast to husband's entire company trying to sell Girl Scout cookies. Was overheard saying: "The teacher is giving little Joshua extra math homework to keep him challenged," and "Oh I can't keep all his playdates straight, he has so many."

The Lady Who Lunches

Every day's a party. Lunch and a little shopping. Maybe a manicure and pedicure. Has a glass of wine at lunch, after all, she's got nowhere to go.

The PTA Princess (aka The Martyr)

Volunteers for every committee because "no one else will". On call to stuff envelopes and clean up the gym after Family Night. Is a room mother five years in a row and always willing to go purchase the teacher gift. Can be counted on to think of creative fund raising ideas and then calligraphy the invitations.

The Granola Guru

Fruit snacks and juice boxes? You're poisoning your kids! Hello! Have you heard of childhood obesity? Only shops at Whole Foods and packs lunches including trail mix and organic milk. Brings wheat free, gluten free, sugar free, carrot cupcakes for a birthday treat.

The Tennis Tart

Pawns off driving carpools and chaperoning field trips due to tennis commitments. When she does show up at school it's in a little tennis outfit with pigtails. Only talks to other tennis tarts.

Selective Hearing

What You Say	What They Hear
No	Maybe
I'll think about it	Yes
Later	Now

Where's the Food Pyramid
When You Need It?

One day when Rachel was four, I was trying to get her to eat her lunch and I actually said, "If you eat your bologna, you can have some ice cream." Huh?

The Lure of the Lunchables

I always feel guilty when I give my kids Lunchables to take to school. (Especially on "Waste Free Wednesday" when they're supposed to bring everything in reusable containers). Even though it comes in its own package, I always put it in a brown paper bag. Like young lovers do with condoms or drunks with whiskey. If the mommy police are volunteering in the lunchroom that day, this will certainly earn me a major citation. "You are accused of knowingly, with intent, giving your child a lunch that is high in fat, calories and sodium." Bad, bad mommy.

But, making lunches EVERY NIGHT is a real drag. And, for some odd-reason, Rachel (picky eater extraordinaire) cannot go a week with the All Star Hot Dogs. So, I continue. But, before you judge me, let me tell you I do have standards. I always take out the can of soda, put in a juice box and tape the package back up. Soda with their school lunch? What kind of

mother do you think I am?

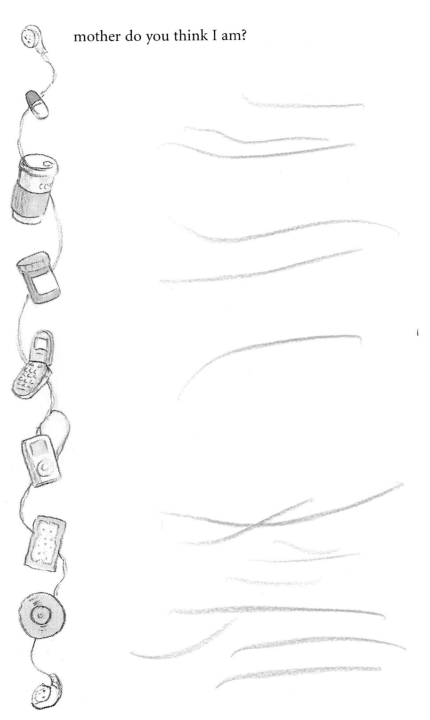

Arlene Schusteff

Parent Proof

For some reason, I cannot master the intricacies of the television. Recording shows and getting to the onscreen TV schedule are beyond me. My kids find this hilarious. One day before leaving for school, Rachel turned every television in the house to the Disney Channel, programmed in a "parental control" code and left. I sat for an hour trying to deprogram the code (and missed a darn good Oprah) before I finally called the cable company. They told me that "for safety reasons" they were not allowed to tell me how to disable the parental controls. Kind of makes you wonder who is controlling who, huh? (And, yes, a long time out and no TV for a week assured me that I wouldn't be stuck watching Lizzie McGuire anytime soon).

Life In Boyville

There's certainly no gender confusion in my family. Jake, is all about speed, dirt and constant motion. He likes skateboards and water parks with dangerously high slides. He does not mind eating dinner with filthy hands and has been known to pick up the last piece of pizza from the floor and shove it in his mouth. If you've ever seen the laundry detergent commercial where the kid rolls around in the mud, slides in the grass and spills grape juice down his shirt, you've pretty much got the picture.

Activities that we both enjoy have always been few and far between. Lately his list of complaints with me is especially long. I don't know how to put together Lego's very well. ("Oh my god, mom, that doesn't look like a bulldozer.") My baseball pitches don't make it over the plate. And, unlike daddy, I cannot recite the lines from every Sponge Bob episode. He'll always be my little boy, but now he's one of them. A male. I'm sure that soon he will be laughing like crazy at The Three Stooges and Monty Python.

Like most things in life, when I look back, there were signs that he was changing from my little boy, to a boy with a capital B. He started refusing to play with girls. Halloween costumes were chosen based on whether or not they came with weapons or fake blood. And, when we went to the bank and the teller offered him a pink lollipop, he said, "Do you have a blue one?"

So, when Jake decided it was time to retire the training wheels from his bike, I wasn't surprised that he wanted his dad to teach him how to ride a two-wheeler. A few minutes after they left to go to the parking lot behind the school to practice, the phone rang. I looked at the caller ID. It was my husband. In the split second before I answered the phone, I envisioned blood, broken bones and fast cars backing out of driveways. "You'll never believe it," he told me,

"He's riding. He's cruising around like he's been doing it for years."

After that, the only thing that Jake wanted to do was ride his bike. All the time. All over the neighborhood. At very fast speeds. He had found his passion. He told me that he was going to be the next Lance Armstrong.

Since I didn't have a bike, this created a problem for me. At first, I walked very quickly behind him, screaming at him to slow down and watch for cars. After a while, I was exhausted. Rachel volunteered to ride with him, but intuition told me she'd dump him in a second if she found a better offer along the way. So, I did what any 43-year old mother would do. I got in the minivan and drove along next to him. (What? Was I supposed to let a six year-old ride around the block by himself?)

Everyday after school, Jake would beg to go for a bike

ride and I would make up an excuse. "After we go to the store," or "just let me put away the laundry." If I put him off long enough, eventually he would find something else to do and I would be off the hook until he asked again and my guilt got the better of me. Then, I'd hop in the van and off we'd go. After a few weeks and a few dozen excuses, I knew something had to change. Most of my friends complained that all their kids wanted to do was play video games and watch television. And here I was, encouraging my son to do just that because it was easier for me.

Since this bike riding thing seemed to be more than a fleeting passion, I decided that I had no choice but to join him. I needed a bike. I drove over to my parents' house and got my old, yellow Schwinn out of their garage. I threw it in the back of the van and drove home. When I put it in the garage next to the kids' shiny new bikes, it looked antiquated. Just like me, I thought. But I certainly wasn't going to invest in a new bike. I was only doing this until Jake got

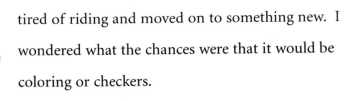

tired of riding and moved on to something new. I wondered what the chances were that it would be coloring or checkers.

A couple days later, Jake and I ventured out for a ride. Okay, I'll admit it was to Starbucks. (If we had to go for a ride, at least it would be to a place where there was coffee waiting for me.) As I got on the bike – was it my imagination or had the seat gotten a lot smaller – I prayed that the old cliché about never forgetting how panned out.

My first few blocks were a bit shaky, but then I gained speed as I tried to keep up with Jake. Memories flashed in my head. Riding to Dairy Queen after a day at the pool. Taking a long ride to the pharmacy to buy candy and Love's So Baby Soft perfume. And riding just for the sake of riding. All over the neighborhood, without hands, racing my friends down the middle of the street and weaving in and out of driveways. I remembered I would dread the day we'd hang the bike from the ceiling in the garage until the cold Chicago winter gave way to spring.

Jake waited impatiently as I finished my coffee. "Want to take a ride to the park and watch the big boys play baseball?" I asked. He looked surprised. "Yeah," he said with a grin. So we rode over and as he watched them, I watched him. No, he wasn't such a little boy anymore. I knew how fast time passed. I knew that one day in the not so distant future he would be embarrassed to be seen riding around town with his mother. Yeah, bike riding. I could definitely do that with him. It would be our thing. It could be worse.

Suddenly, I noticed that Jake had pedaled over to the skate park to watch the skateboarders and I joined him. "Hey, little dude," one of them called to him, "want to try it?" "Yeah," he said, jumping off his bike and letting it slam to the ground. And before I could say Lance Armstrong, he was off.

Halloween: It's the New Christmas

What the hell has happened to Halloween? It's as though someone pumped it full of steroids and let it loose. It used to be that you could throw a sheet over your head, grab a grocery bag and go run around the neighborhood until your bag was full.

I remember when I was eight. I donned a black leotard, ears and a powder puff on my rear end and went as a Playboy bunny. (Talk about politically incorrect).

Now, the day after school starts, the Halloween pressure starts to simmer.

The catalogs arrive with their costumes and customized pumpkin bags. Empty stores are converted into Halloween stores with names like "Halloween Village". The school supplies are cleaned out and the candy and Styrofoam tombstones are moved in. Your daughter decides to be a hippie-dancer-witch girl.

You remember last year you went to the store to buy a costume on September 27th and your son had a fit because all the good costumes with knives and guns were already gone.

On the big day, you call in sick, knowing your childless by choice boss will not understand this "new Halloween". You know that if your kids don't see you at the school parade, they'll be talking about you in therapy ten years from now.

On Halloween, for the first time in 30 years, it's 85 degrees. The extra warm costumes you bought have them crying and complaining. They ditch them and change into shorts.

If you're really lucky, you get to stay home and hand out the candy while your husband chases after them as they run house to house, reminding them repeatedly to "say thank you."

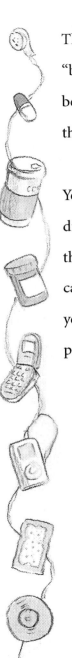

They come home hot and sweaty, arguing who got "better" candy. It takes an hour to get them to bed because surprisingly old-looking "kids" keep ringing the doorbell. Once they're asleep, the real fun starts.

You and your husband pour a glass of wine and you dig into the candy. You feel cheap when you realize that most of your neighbors handed out full-size candy bars and you only sprung for the minis. Then you notice the six Hershey Bars and tear open a wrapper. Maybe this new Halloween isn't so bad after all.

My Porn

I hoard them. I'm obsessed with them. They're next to my bed, in the family room and on the floor of the minivan. I never let the kids cut them up for school projects. I look at them over and over, studying the glossy photos intently. I suspect that periodically my husband secretly takes them out to the recycling bin and buries them under week-old newspapers.

Decorating catalogs are my porn. I can't resist the color-coordinated perfect rooms with plump pillows and furniture that doesn't look like it needs a good shot of Febreze.

I love them all: Pottery Barn, Crate & Barrel, Ballard Designs, Restoration Hardware. You name it , chances are I get it. I know the rooms by heart. "Oh, they added a new coffee table", or "Wow, now that slipcover comes in pumpkin velvet."

I lust after the rooms. I just know that if I had the perfect sectional sofa with the leather ottoman in the middle, life would be grand. We'd relax on the beautiful sofa, eating a big bowl of popcorn and watching a classic movie. I try to block out the thought that I'd probably be yelling at the kids not to get popcorn kernels all over the new sofa as they fought over control of the remote. But a mom can dream, can't she?

Magazine Makeovers

Before Kids	After Kids
Real Simple	Simply Unorganized
House Beautiful	House Bearable
Us	Us & Them
In Style	Dressed and Showered
Woman's Day	Woman's Morning, Noon & Night
Bon Appetit	Just Eat!
Cooking Light	Cooking, yeah!
More	Gimme
Metropolitan Hom	Suburban Home
People	Little People

Reality Television, Mom Style

Who needs bachelors, biggest losers and survivors?

You've got your own reality.

The Amazing Race

Watch with amazement as one mother gets two kids to five different birthday parties, a soccer game, and a doctor's appointment without once screaming, "If you don't stop it, I'm turning this car around."

Survivor

The parent still coherent after a week-long driving trip touring historical sights of the Midwest with the entire family in minivan with a broken air conditioner and a dog with the runs.

Extreme Makeover: Home Edition

Can the house be put back together after a thunderstorm forces the playgroup indoors to finger paint, play hide and seek and consume large amounts of sugar?

Lost

Is it really possible to lose your shoes, backpack, and lunch box on the first day of school? Our talented first-grader shows you how.

The O.C. – (aka as The Over-Committed)
After going to over-committers anonymous, one mother feels stigmatized by the PTA mothers after she refuses to participate in any bake sales or sell wrapping paper and cookie dough for the rest of the year.

The Surreal Life
This un-edited documentary follows the trials and tribulations of one couple as they bring baby home from the hospital and wonder "now what?" Be sure not to miss mom's breakdown when she realizes that it now takes her three hours to leave the house and she is unable to shave both her legs on the same day.

7th Heaven
After breaking up with her boyfriend, the teenager

next door calls and asks to start babysitting for you "as much as possible."

Alias

When the volunteer list reaches you at open house, you smile and sign up for everything...under the name June Cleaver.

Wife Swap

After husband asks you "what you do all day" you resolve to get yourself swapped with another mother to show him just how good he has it.

48 Hours

How long can the wet towel sit on the bathroom floor before anyone picks it up? Short on drama, long on suspense, you'll be riveted to the TV.

No Truth, Just Dare

Go Ahead, I dare you to…

Go to Target and leave with only what you went in for.

Drive in the car with the kids eating McDonald's French fries without stealing a few.

Drive directly past everyone in the carpool line and go straight to the front.

Go into Starbucks and when the barista asks what you'd like, say "coffee".

Wear the painted macaroni and yarn necklace to work and keep it on all day.

When you're at a party and someone asks what you do, look them in the eye and say, "I'm the CEO of my household."

The Costco Capers

Ever try and squeeze in just one more errand to save you some time the next day? I used to, until the day I almost had a nervous breakdown at Costco. Let the following tale of misery be a warning to you, don't do it!

I pick the kids up at school and decide to go straight to Costco. I know if we go home first, I'll never get them out of the house again. I have no snacks and no drinks. (In other words, I'm asking for trouble). I have half an hour to shop before Rachel needs to be at ballet.

As soon as we walk in the store, the kids beg me to push them on a flatbed cart. Thinking they'll be "contained" I agree, forgetting their combined weight is over 160 pounds and I haven't worked out in seven years.

We pass the candy aisle (Why do they put it up front?) They're hungry and can they please split a ten pound bag of Skittles? No, I say. Can they go to the snack bar? No, I say again. No time. I send them off to look for free food samples while I race around fighting with the flatbed to stay straight. Jake finds me and shows me his find, a cup full of tiny red bits that he thinks are candy.

Before I can warn him, he puts the entire contents in his mouth. Except, it's not candy, it's a cup full of Bacon Bits. He spits them all out in my hand. No garbage in sight. I'm not surprised.

Now I'm pushing a flatbed with one hand and holding his regurgitated "candy" in the other. At this point, I'm halfway through my list. I've go ten minutes to spare when Rachel says she has to pee. Trying to put "Stranger Danger" out of my mind, I send her alone. I'll race around, get the rest of the stuff and meet her at the register. I ask her to please, please get

me a tissue for the Bacon Bits.

Sweating bullets, I finally have everything. Rachel is standing at the register. I breathe a sigh of relief. Then I see her hands are empty, no tissue. Damn. She refuses to go back, telling me the bathroom smells "nasty."

The line inches along. I should've left minutes ago. The slowest cashier on the face of the earth checks us out. I ask her for a tissue. She hands me a receipt and finally, a tissue. I throw the Bacon Bits out and shove the receipt in my purse.

We race to the front door and I tell them again that we have no time to stop for a jumbo hot dog. There's another line of people, all waiting to exit. They're all showing their receipts to prove they paid for the 87 pack of paper towels. I reach in my purse. No receipt. The kids never saw the receipt. How did I lose the receipt in 60 seconds?

I'm now ten minutes behind. Class starts in four minutes and the ballet teacher "frowns on tardiness." Despite my whiny children and assurances that I paid, the guard will not let us exit. He tells me I need to go to customer service and show my membership card and they'll give me a duplicate receipt. The kids are really whining now. I leave them with the cart and run to customer service.

The lady in front of me was overcharged 16 cents on a bag of clementines and is waiting for a refund. I start thinking about "Stranger Danger" again. But then I hear them fighting. Loudly. I finally get the receipt and race back. The guard studies it as if I'm pulling a fast one over on him. I throw the boxes in the trunk and race to the ballet studio. I am 27 minutes late and the teacher shoots me daggers when I open the door to let Rachel in.

Later when I get home and open the trunk of the van, the bag of potatoes rolls out and lands on my foot. I

reach down to pick them up and find Bacon Bits all over them and a receipt on the driveway.

I couldn't make this stuff up, really.

The Ten Second Test of Friendship Compatibility

"There's going to be a snow day today. No school."

Quick, what's your first thought?

When Rachel was in kindergarten, we had a horrible snowstorm. Horrible enough for the school to decide on Wednesday that they were going to cancel school for the remainder of the week.

I was one of the moms who volunteered to do the phone tree if school was ever cancelled. (Which, of course, had not happened since anyone could remember, the main reason I took the job.)

I started calling at 6:30 am. Even in their groggy state, a number of moms were clearly thrilled with the news. "We can go sledding," and "Great, no carpools," some told me. Others were not so happy. "Oh my god, do you think Blockbuster will be open?" One suddenly alert mom said, "I was dreading your call."

It occurred to me later that all of my closest friends are in the second group. I'm not surprised.

Arlene Schusteff

Lies You Tell Yourself and Others

We don't care whether it's a boy or a girl as long as it's healthy.

We're proud that he's in touch with his feminine side. Many experts say it's completely normal for a ten year-old boy to put on his mom's high heels and makeup.

As long as he's happy, we don't care if he's a ditch digger or a doctor.

Its okay you struck out six times. As long as you tried your best.

You're kidding, you're pregnant? I couldn't tell at all. You look great.

Sign of the Times

Before entering the library, please turn off all cell phones, iPods, beepers, and any electronic game devices.

Modern Mom Sing-Along

The Mommy is in Hell

(to the tune of The Farmer in the Dell)

The mommy is in hell, the mommy is in hell,

Oh no, the kids are sick, the mommy is in hell.

The mommy needs a break, the mommy needs a

    break,

Oh no, the kids are sick, please say it's a big mistake.

The mommy is in hell, the mommy is in hell,

Oh no, the kids are sick, now Daddy is as well.

Take Me Out To the Day Spa

(to the tune of Take Me Out to the Ballgame)

Take me out to the day spa,

Take me out to the spa,

Buy me some pampering and polishing,

Kids are with dad and betcha they're hollering,

'Cuz it's roots, roots, roots that are showing,

If I don't touch up it's lame,

Then its 1-2-3 strikes hello to the mommy

hall of shame.

How Much is That iPod in the Window?

(to the tune of How Much is that Doggie in the Window?)

How much is that iPod in the window?

The one that I really need bad.

How much is that iPod in the window?

Buy it or else I'll get mad.

Stressed-Out Family

(to the tune of the Barney theme song)

I love you, you love me, but we're a stressed out family

With a great big schedule and way too much to do

We're just trying to make it through.

Let's Give Them Something to Talk About...

Out with the girls and tired of talking about pre-school registration and ear infections? Here's a mom's list of hot topics, sure to get the conversation rolling.

Would you rather have one child with lice or three children with the stomach flu?

You're going out for an elegant dinner. Who would you rather have choose your outfit, your mother-in-law or 12 year old daughter?

Would your rather have a live-in housekeeper or be a size two?

Which would you rather live without, your cell phone or your microwave?

You can get rid of one chore for the rest of your life. Will it be making beds, making meals, or making love?

Your neighbor asks you to collect her mail while she's on vacation. Her People magazine comes wrapped in plastic. Do you open it and read it?

Mommy, What's Erectile Dysfunction and Will You Buy Me One?

Words our mothers never had to explain to us:

Surrogate mother

Terrorist attack

Trans fat

Brazilian

Botox

Boob Job

Why I Deserve a Sticker...

Got every place on time and had enough snacks and Gatorade for everyone in the carpool.

Made it to the bottom of the laundry basket and folded and hung up all the clothes.

Didn't skip any words when forced to read *Amazing Rescue Vehicles* for the third time that night. Asked thought provoking questions.

Didn't flip off the mother who wedged her enormous SUV in front of me in the carpool line. Smiled, waved, and backed up to let her in.

Didn't say a word when nine year-old daughter walked out of the house with a face full of pretend makeup. Yelled encouragement…"You look great!"

Bringing Up Girlie-Girl

"Mom, you said that we could go shopping for back-to-school clothes after breakfast. It's after breakfast."

I turned away from my stack of paperwork recently and took a good look at my daughter. She was dressed in flared jeans, a ribbed tank top and platform flip-flops.

Be careful what you wish for, I thought, remembering how excited I was to learn my baby was, yes, indeed, a girl. How I envisioned dressing her in cute, little matching outfits with lace and bows in her hair. What I didn't picture was sweet baby Rachel actually having an opinion about what she wore and when she wore it.

At 18 months, she still had no hair on her head, and I had grown tired of people asking me how old my little boy was. So I took to dressing her in very

feminine clothes and sticking a frilly band on her bald, little head. We even have a framed picture of her wearing her first dress.

Now, years later, every day is just another shopping opportunity waiting to happen for my fashionista.

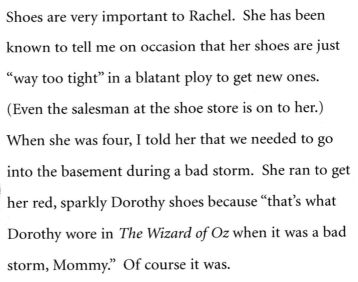

Shoes are very important to Rachel. She has been known to tell me on occasion that her shoes are just "way too tight" in a blatant ploy to get new ones. (Even the salesman at the shoe store is on to her.) When she was four, I told her that we needed to go into the basement during a bad storm. She ran to get her red, sparkly Dorothy shoes because "that's what Dorothy wore in *The Wizard of Oz* when it was a bad storm, Mommy." Of course it was.

I vaguely remember being her age – not so cute and definitely not so fashionable. I know this because I've seen more than one picture of myself dressed in Sears Toughskins (with double reinforced knees, no less) and a grimy Cubs sweatshirt, long hair hanging in my face. And I can honestly say (my mother corroborates) that I don't remember caring about what I wore until I was in high school.

On the other hand, I have a friend who complains that her daughter only wears jeans and sloppy t-shirts that are two sizes too big. I can see how this would be a problem as well (albeit a cheaper, less nerve-wracking one.) Besides, I know that I probably indulge her. Ultimately, I am the one that buys her these things, right? But maybe it's because I do remember being 16 (arguably a little older than ten) and going back-to-school shopping with my own mother. She wanted things that "would last" and outfits that were "practical." I yearned for a closet full of Calvin Klein jeans that would show the world how cool I was.

Some, including my husband, have been known to say that Rachel has learned how to work me over to get what she wants in the clothes department. She

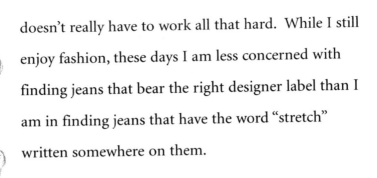

doesn't really have to work all that hard. While I still enjoy fashion, these days I am less concerned with finding jeans that bear the right designer label than I am in finding jeans that have the word "stretch" written somewhere on them.

So, we went shopping. And, as we were taking a break in the food court, I noticed two teenage girls at the next table. They appeared to be about 15. They were dressed in tight jeans, belly shirts and platform shoes. They had multiple earrings in each ear and a stud in their bellybuttons for good measure. They were drinking cappuccinos and discussing "how lame" it was to be here shopping with their moms (who evidently were still off paying for their purchases.) Rachel noticed them as well. "Hey mom, do you think it hurts to get your belly button pierced?" she asked.

I saw my future flash before me. One day shopping would be the least of my worries. "Hey, Rachel,"

I said. "Let's go get a new headband and shoes to wear with your jeans."

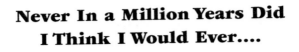

Never In a Million Years Did
I Think I Would Ever....

Spend part of an evening debating who is prettier, Pocahontas or Ariel, the Little Mermaid.

Try to get a "stuck doody" out of my kid's rear end.

Have an argument with my husband about how many actors have played Barney since the show started. (And then do a Google search to try and find out!)

Think of going to the bathroom as "me time."

Law of Gravity

Our evening when Rachel was about four, she came into my bedroom while I was getting undressed.

When I took off my bra, she pointed to my chest and said, "I thought your boobs were supposed to be up higher. How come yours are flopping down by your belly?"

Proud Moment

Rachel (age four) to a woman in line at the bank:

"I really like your tie-dye hair and the way the top part is black and the bottom is white. And, how do you get it to stick up so high?"

Anatomy 101

Jake (age five) at a Bar Mitzvah service, loudly:

How come you have a butt crack by your boobs?

Actual Conversation

With Jake, age seven

Me: The garbage lady is here.

Him: You mean the man?

Me: No, it's a lady.

Him: The man?

Me: No, the lady with the red hair.

Him: She can't be a garbage man.

Me: Why?

Him: She's not a man.

Me: Ladies can be garbage people too.

Him: No, they can't.

Me: Ladies and girls can do anything boys and men can do. Just like boys and men can do anything.

Him: Well, why would a man want to have a baby? That's why he told God to have his wife do it.

My Family

When I went to Rachel's kindergarten parent-teacher conference, the teacher handed me a packet of her work.

Inside was a sheet titled "My Family." It read:

Daddy: Likes to play with me.

Jake: Likes trucks.

Mommy: Likes to talk on the phone and eat food in her bed.

Actual Conversation

With Rachel, age nine

8:30 am

Me: Wear a coat, its cold.

Her: No, I don't need one.

Me;   You're gonna be cold.

Her: No, I'm not.

Me;   You are.

Her: I'm not wearing a coat.

Me: Fine. Freeze.

Her: Fine.

3:15 pm

Her: Oh my god! Why didn't you tell me to wear a coat? I was freezing at recess. If I get sick it's going to be your fault!

Little Kids, Little Problems...

My friends with teenagers are quick to tell me,
"little kids, little problems; big kids, big problems."
I can only imagine…

Now	Then
Refuses to go to bed	Refuses to wake up
Gazes into your eyes	Rolls her eyes.
Teething ring	Belly ring
Runs everywhere	Refuses to walk anywhere
Will only wear one outfit	Changes her outfit three times a day
Begs you to sing a song	Begs you not to sing

Now	**Then**
Walks around naked	Screams if you walk in her room while she's changing
You tiptoe while she's sleeping	Need a bullhorn to wake her up
Constantly asks why not	Constantly asks why not

New Mom vs. Old Mom

Toys

New Mom: Always educational. Lots of pieces

Old Mom: Refuses to buy anything that makes noise
or moves

Fast Food

New Mom: Have you seen the statistics on childhood
obesity?

Old Mom: Knows every value meal number by heart.

Babysitter

New Mom: Checks references, spies on with hidden
camera.

Old Mom: Asks ten year-old walking her dog if she
will sit on Saturday night.

Birthday Party

New Mom: Plans six months in advance. Costs more
than your wedding.

Old Mom: Writes a check and goes to Chuck E. Cheese.

Carpool

New Mom: Checks to make sure car seat was installed properly and discreetly asks others about driving record.

Old Mom: You've got room? Great, can she go with you?

Lunch

New Mom: Peanut butter and jelly on whole wheat bread cut into cute shapes with cookie cutter.

Old Mom: Peanut butter (out of jelly) on white bread with no crust.

Video

New Mom: Rarely turns on a video.

Old Mom: The longer, the better. Content not important.

"Mommy Speak"

So, you learned a foreign language in high school?
Here's something much more valuable, a crash course
in Mommy Speak.

What they say:	What they think:
Does he need a tissue?	Is he sick?
He has so much energy.	He's such a wild animal.
He's going to be a football player.	God is he fat.
He's so sweet.	He must be gay.
Did he pick out his own outfit?	You let him wear that?
She speaks so well.	Does she ever shut up?

What they say:	**What they think:**
You sure have your hands full.	I'm so glad I'm not you.
Does he need a hat?	You incompetent mother.
Be careful jumping on that couch.	Were you raised in a barn?

Actual Conversation

2:00 am

Jake: (yelling) Mom, mom, come in my room. I need you!

Me: (Rushing into his room) What's wrong?

Jake: I was just thinking, how exactly do I find a good wife?

So What

Jake's friend: My picture is better.

Jake:(at age three) My picture is better.

Jake's friend: No, it's not.

Jake: Yes, it is.

Jake's friend: Well, I'm faster than you are.

Jake: No, I am.

Jake's friend: My dad is way faster than your dad.

Jake: So what, my dad has the fattest tummy in the
whole class.

Don't Ask, Don't Tell

When Rachel turned ten, I knew it was probably time to have some kind of conversation with her about the "changes" she'd soon be experiencing.

She wanted nothing to do with it, telling me "not to talk to her about gross stuff."

I didn't push it and instead bought her an age appropriate book. She took one look at the cover and said, "Please return that and get me a Mary-Kate and Ashley book instead."

But later that day, I noticed the book on her desk. I figured she'd read it when she was ready.

About a week later, we were having dinner and we started talking about our day. Rachel gave me the usual one-word grunts when I asked about school. Frustrated, Howard said, "Did you learn anything

today, Rachel?" Without missing a beat she replied, "Well after reading the book mom gave me, I know that I don't want to be getting public hair anytime soon."

(No, that was not a typo!)

The Stone Age

Rachel (age nine): I'm bored.

Me: Why don't you read a book, or do an art project, or watch a DVD?

Rachel: Those are boring.

Me: Then go outside and jump on the trampoline or ride your bike.

Rachel: I'm not in the mood to go outside.

Me: Well, then help me unload the dishwasher.

Rachel: No, I want to do something fun.

Me (irritated): Listen, when I was growing up we didn't have CD players or trampolines in the backyard. So don't tell me you're bored.

Rachel: Oh my god! It's not my fault that you were poor in the olden days. Why are you getting mad at me?

Go Ask Your Father...

Questions I Still Don't Know the Answer to:

Why do your fingers get wrinkly in the bathtub?

How does the remote turn on the TV?

If everyone pees in the pool at the same time, will the water turn yellow?

Is there a swear toe?

How does the aspirin know if you have a headache or a sprained ankle?

You Gotta Have Friends

Paige (Rachel's friend, age ten): Arlene, will you put me in your book?

Me: I don't know, Paige. I can't really put all Rachel's friends in my book.

Paige: Please, once I said something really, really funny.

Me: What did you say?

Paige: Well, when I was little, I asked my mom if I could make a wish to the Diaper Genie.

Me: That is funny! Just don't tell all the other girls I put you in, okay?

Paige: Don't worry, I can keep a secret. And besides, Rachel told me that the book isn't really that funny, so probably no one's going to read it anyway.

Afterword

I hope you enjoyed reading about my adventures in motherhood. You were so nice to read my stories. I'd love to hear yours (that's only fair, right?). Drop me a line at Arlene@ArleneSchusteff.com. I love reader feedback and besides, it makes me feel better to know that other people's kids are as high maintenance as mine. Also, be sure and bookmark my website, ArleneSchusteff.com for more mom humor and to find out whether I ever kicked my Starbucks habit and began shopping at Costco again.

 Arlene Schusteff lives in a suburb of Chicago with her husband, Howard, and two children, Rachel, 10 and Jake, 7. Her work has appeared in the *Chicago Tribune*, *LA Times*, *Family Fun*, *SHOP, etc.*, *Chicago Parent* and a host of other magazines, newspapers and websites. Arlene also writes a column for the Pioneer Press newspapers called A Mom Thing.